Flageolets at the Bazaar
Judith Lal

Smith/Doorstop Books

Published 2007 by
Smith/Doorstop Books
The Poetry Business
The Studio
Byram Arcade
Westgate
Huddersfield HD1 1ND

Copyright © Judith Lal 2007
All Rights Reserved

ISBN 978-1-902382-92-7
Typeset at The Poetry Business
Printed by Swiftprint, Huddersfield

The Poetry Business gratefully acknowledges the help of Arts Council England and Kirklees Metropolitan Council.

Acknowledgements
Her poems have been published in *Aesthetica, The New Writer, The North, Poetry London*, and *Reactions2*.
She won first prize in *The New Writer* competition (poetry collection category).

This collection was a winner in The Poetry Business
Book & Pamphlet Competition 2006

CONTENTS

5	Midnight In The World's Call Centre
7	The Parting Of Plates
8	Finding Nothing
9	The World's Oldest Pudding
10	The Kingfisher's Gift
12	Dunes Of Starlings
14	Lesser Spotted Woodpecker
15	Deer
16	The Walk
17	Hare
18	Bonus Of 13 Bohemian Waxwings
19	Kestrel
20	The Singer From Pakistan Addresses An English Audience For The First Time
21	Finches
22	Goldfinches
23	Swallowtail Day
24	Kandinsky And The Kingfisher
25	Red
26	Drought
28	Barn Owl Hunting In July
29	Squall
30	A Year On
31	The Butterfly Tree

For Dad with love

MIDNIGHT IN THE WORLD'S CALL CENTRE

*Across the subcontinent as a whole it is estimated that
partition resulted in over a million deaths.*

Summer bowing out through kitchen
door makes lotus flamed candles
dervish. Much depends upon listening
to your stories, my birth. Scheherazade.
Arabian nights reversed. As long as a

piece of cotton that goes into the making
of one thousand and one sarees. They always
start with a spinning wheel fathering words;
a coloured mandala spoked and spoken,
turning, as history turns in its booked bed.

Putting a spin on politics would be a
good one if only there were newspapers
posted to one thousand and one ripped
midnights. 1947, the sun is a golden
pheasant shaking out its feathers, no

newspapers, but a scream fireworked
off from neighbouring village
makes India a house on fire.

To remap a country you need
blackboard, white chalk,
blood coloured blood. Cows.

Cows strapped to the line and the
patience of cows to wait for a train not
to show, the time it takes a beard to grow.

And even if it does come through, cannot
stop because the headless driver is in
a hurry to get his carriages of the massacred
fast away from anywhere here.

You survive, it does not come
to having your trousers pulled down
to see if you are circumcised.
Brahman, *Musalman*, beggarman, thief.

But try telling this poem it should not
be here and it will fold itself into
a paper boat, sail in milk and flowers,

offering a candle upon the tears of
Ganga as they sluice and slug years
to beach in the now of my kitchen table.

THE PARTING OF PLATES

An earthquake in Kashmir,
the partition of plates,
the way history is made of
other peoples tears, the taste
of salt that Mahatma asked
the sea for. There are the plates
fissured and fudged that slide
under the earth and the plates
that have no foodstuff on and the
plates that are family heirlooms,
keepsafes no longer safe,
some broken in the hurry
to pack for the rest of this life.

FINDING NOTHING

After a year of headaches
they scanned
your head.

After a week
they said they
had found nothing.

Just like ancient Indian
mathematicians
finding a positive

discovery of
negatives.
Philosophy of zilch.

An abacus with
neither debt nor
fortune.

A hoop of zero,
birthing bubbles
which burst,

as your life
rounds up all
its equations into

some sum Nirvana.
The finding of nothing.

THE WORLD'S OLDEST PUDDING

Birds announce that the
milkman is coming with
the sweet cream of
Krishna's milking.

Statuette tears of pearly rice,
a live wire of saffron,
dessertspoon of rose water,
silver leaf scree,

is what you ate
three full moons
after a homebirth,

or at temple,
and home again,
after the hospital

lets you out with
79 years
under loose belt.

THE KINGFISHER'S GIFT

There has always been
someone to share
the kingfisher with
or

mostly it has always been
that someone else sees it
and points it out,

hands up to the blue,
to feel that bullet of wonderment
take a bite. Again. Still.

A boy from a hotel in Sri Lanka,
or my mother in The Cotswolds
by quick witted water,

but now that I'm in
none of those places
I walk thinking that

the wind has dropped back to the start,
he may get to see fish
swim the other side of the mirror,

I may get to see him throw
his precious stones into the mirror,
and then the sound,

the sound of a hungry
old man playing his
piccolo too madly,
but he doesn't care, the air

loves him beyond anything right now,
as he loves the air.
He gives it his colours in
a fulgid tear.

DUNES OF STARLINGS

A low ceiling on the season,
expect sounds of the sea
but get wind quietly talking
into their swish leaf-feathers.

First thought of as large groups,
are small groups,
rivulets in shrimping sky
coalesce over marsh into

blown dunes of uncountable dark bees
practising their smart geometry
as an ever changing
fingerprint upon evening.

Starlings that imitate ringtones by day
take the shape of a whale at 6 o'clock.
So glad to have it fed
with cake crumb plankton.

Now a bird of prey rises
from a place only she knows of,
a stab to the whale
turns it into something else.

They go on being beautiful
and knowing nothing of it,
until the leafless trees
conduct their music down

to a trickle, to lie in
the cool mud-cot of earth,
to watch that mirrorball

turn bird and star
and star and bird.

LESSER SPOTTED WOODPECKER

Lesser spotted is spotted less but
all day he has purred sharply into
alders, does not fear himself as small
or first up this dark tower block,
flattering the day's chrysalis to open.

The tree undoes its knot, lends him
an ear to fall on. This is his tough
living, not knowing what he is
looking for until he has found
it. Once found, he remembers

and starts out in toothsome
wind to look for it all over again.
Everyday the dropped and caught
feather of memory. It is not sex
(it's still early and too cold)

nor death (nobody has ever told him
there are only 3000 of his kind)
but on he goes, drumming along
the bright branch of my mind.
Music on the bone.

DEER

December. Trees hold up their
empty baskets to the skies.
You walk upon the concreted
river with the only other warm
bloodied creature. Not only one

now but three, all following their
soft currants down to a saucer of
water which they nibble so delicately
on. Here, if the wind is right you
can get close, hold the glass up to
your eye. Inside

circles of glass are Indian eyes,
lashes clean with soot, face like
a walk with Modigliani's pencil
and legs not as Sita saw *set with
precious stones* but of the most
elegantly wrapped bone

now footfalling up wild shires of air.
Your loneliness has a strong smell
to her who is never lonely as long as there
are trees, even the most dead ones.

THE WALK

Today she will go for a walk
alone. She knows the dangers,
women have been raped and

killed for less, or kept
alive in front of their children
on a day equally as beautiful.

Yet how one foot goes on after the other,
dragooned over the rainbowed puddle
and past the flytipped mattress.

Wiping her legs together above the fields
or as someone said *giving a declaration
to dependence upon the earth.*

And the green woodpecker flies away
startled but not frightened, laughing out
loud from his burnished pages.

HARE

In newly saved light the hare jumps
from his brown box of a field.
Ears are only the half of it.

Pariah in the rude health of
golden louché patchwork.
There are no edges to the
pictures he makes

with eyes that let in everything, yes
even snow, and here is the calling
of dark milky clouds,
a storm comes by in impressive
tea-cups. The weather bombs.

O that which I wouldn't do to stay
by this bony field
to watch the enjambment his large accurate feet
make running into tomorrow.

I know it will be hard as horizontal rain,
but I have a wish to join the hare in his big eatery
where one never feels grateful or guilty.

BONUS OF 13 BOHEMIAN WAXWINGS

Not that you can tell
until you hear them speaking in bells *sirrrrrrr*
but they all seem fatly happy on one lamppost in suburbia

that would mean nothing unless you lived there,
which they do,
over the random roundabouts

of an undone Russian wedding ring
in Dussendale ghost-written
by a child to Dustbindale. Inspired.

Plump belly up to the berry bearing universe
is a favourite locus
to sun-tip their tails.

When the crocus opens its samite egg-cup
and the birds have eaten their weight
a hundred times over in rubies,

feathers dipped in red sealing wax
break open and the 13 triangular
letters fly the Silk Route back.

KESTREL

Finally becoming tired of everything
looking like something else
and after two glasses of red,

it's time to take each other
down to the undressed water
showing fallow curves in March.

Every river is sacred from East Anglia to
East Asia. *One river, one mu-ther,*
how the word looks different in the air.
How water takes ashes and pollen as its brocade

and everything looks like something
else in this dusky puzzle. You decide
on it being a dung heap with a kestrel on,
then I, an uprooted tree with a kestrel on.

A kestrel for sure,
stoking pebbles in her breast
or laundering a kill,
readying feathers

that we are not yet close
enough to get under
before well executed flight.

THE SINGER FROM PAKISTAN ADDRESSES AN ENGLISH AUDIENCE FOR THE FIRST TIME

Raising money for the Kashmir Earthquake Appeal
he sings Allah O.
It does something to his face,

a raga vowel that raises cheekbones.
Spotlit rain and sun troughs
collect in skin dimples.

*This song is about
my eyes are like swords.*

*This song is
we dance together and you win.*

*And this song is
I wait for …*

Pause.

I wait for …

Turns to the harmonium player, looks for the word there.

What? I wait for what?

Your beloved she prompts.

Yes, my beloved.

He looks into his voice-box and finds something new.

*This song is
I wait for my beloved.*

FINCHES

That summer, water found its way into politics
and a pollen-cloud blew in from another country
to settle on bodywork as if thinking of no better
place to start a meadow. Then names appeared,
written in saffron and in love with other names.

The bath emptied of gentle volumes (along with
whatever babies had their beginnings in it) onto
cornflowers and thistles that creep on in burgundy.
And if you went quickly into the garden, without
a thought or much fuss, finches would put a song

on the bubble and refuse to fly from it, even
singing down to the cat, but if you went slowly,
thinking them up as you went, they would cut
all ties with your heart. Because of this they made
themselves dear, especially him with a face like

a blindfolded rose, and legs like divining sticks,
little warrior clutching the saucer of water I put
on the ground and by way of drinking makes a gift of.

GOLDFINCHES

A charm of goldfinches visit when I'm not home.
They pull cobwebs from my door saying,

we who represent the infinite riches of heaven,
called by today and found you not in,
it is a pity we missed you.

I imagine they sound like Kathmandu.

SWALLOWTAIL DAY

Kerchiefs pulled one by one from the
east sleeve of this island, wet silk in
a slow breeze over fens. A swallowtail
skips either side of the solstice,
interrupted only by a wolf spider,
whose web is like the sugared string
of a musical instrument come loose as
day is played over half way through.
Brings down lucky coloured plectrum
to sleep lightly in a thin hammock.
It doesn't know what to do with
the pompadour boutique eyes
brightly brushed with red shadows,
the war make-up of a Hindi Goddess
that stares out dreams, or its tail like an
inked comma that comes after the word death.

KANDINSKY AND THE KINGFISHER

He heard colour before he saw it,
much like us here in the evening
palette of June, listening out for
a blinding cocktail of pigments
that eventually arrive towards
the kind of imperial blue that gets
scales all lined up the right way to be
stroked down by the insides of throats.

RED

Sameer Shah the dashing young
dentist and natural stand in for the
wayward hero who goes down with a bout
of something, takes one look at my tooth
as though looking at *Chomolungma*
pushing her wisdom up between India
and China and says, *Your name, it means
Red. Open a little wider please.* In response
I cannot help but bite the mirror. The
Victorians thought it always a healthy
colour to have next to skin. I imagine
the women waving off husbands who get
smaller and ever smaller in tweed and
singlets until disappearing up into white out,
into the lamasery of the snows, while they
stay home in underwear that contrary to
popular belief was red as red you like.

DROUGHT

Sun like burning ghee.
Milk already buttering.
Toes browning,

you move the chillies on through
the garden's clockwork shadows,
lips hung to dry.

The rose asks for a glass of water,
no cloud snagged on its thorns
for forty days and even more nights.

The heat, that giant blue butterfly
resting on mustard fields,
quarrying a wetted light,

beating its wings wingless,
a shivering caravan of prayer flags,
desert festooned.

The blown glass ships of
Galileo's Thermometer
have sunk.

The lake
has left its bed
of broken pottery.

A friend rings to say
she is having a child
in December.

You pray, *Oh god, let there
be water in various shapes
between us now and then.*

BARN OWL HUNTING IN JULY

Love pulls the strings of this feather
fan, sending little lizards back over

the edge. The breeze concertinaed
in and out over a field so tindered

that anything left could only
wish upon midday to crawl under

the moon, back its weight with the
slow metal chain of their pulse.

He doesn't seem to think so,
he will do this for as long

as it takes, he leaves the
hours drying. Dust is on fire

at the tips of his wings.
Even the sun may take its eye

off the Perseid ball of his life,
fall to sleep watching waves,

all proper white, rolling the
peaks of his hunger until he

can return the valentine of
his face and the flower of

another creature's heart to
owlets so choked up with love.

SQUALL

First you see a spider go into one,
park up on a bit of bed-sick ceiling.
Some gutsy deity sucks on the curtains.
Then your lover gets a nose bleed
just as those first slap-happy
drops meet with the street.

Finally rain like unbroken horses.
You go to each room thinking
you're sure it's coming down
a little harder from this one,
seeing dragonfly dash lightning
from a mantle of Krishna indigo,

and seeing the birdbath's
slip-glaze restored in another.

A YEAR ON

They claimed never to have got the
certificate she sent, so were very sorry
but held her accountable for all of his debts.

So she walked to the council with
his ashes like the stuff of teabags ripped,
made a pyramid infusion of tooth, nail, bone,

on the desk. To prove real as life, that he
was most dead, to prove she didn't need their
offered cup and much less their sympathy.

THE BUTTERFLY TREE

So hot, salt finds a way to the surface
of skin and in The Great Wood
the wind is a snake in the canopy.

A tree leaks from its side showing
that underneath it only wears a dress
of spun saliva. Butterflies in

residual holi colours stop by at its
openings, exist on nothing but tears.
Some no bigger than a postage stamp

probe gobbets of sugar, demarcated
with blobs of mother-of-pearl on
underside. Some make the most

with eyes of perfectly fitted jet
which sends light packing at over
a hundred different angles. They

all fly away in small boatloads with
calligraphy written on their wings,
to be made into an alphabet by a

man who pins then to the page
with owlish eyes and god given ease.